THE CAT IN THE HAT DICTIONARY

By Dr. Seuss

Illustrated by P.D. Eastman

Collins

An imprint of HarperCollinsPublishers

ISBN 1 84 509308 9

© 1964 by Random House Inc. All Rights Reserved
A Beginner Book published by arrangement with Random House Inc., New York, USA
First published in the UK 1965. This revised paperback edition published in the UK 2002 by
HarperCollins*Children's Books,* a division of HarperCollins*Publishers* Ltd.
This edition produced in 2005 for Bookmart Ltd, Blaby Road, Wickston, Leicester LE18 4SE
Registered number 2372865

The HarperCollins website address is:
www.**harpercollinschildrensbooks**.co.uk

Printed and bound in China by
SNP Lee Fung Ltd

About this book

This madcap dictionary is full of ridiculous alligators, foolish bears and giraffes' uncles, all racing around and getting involved in nonsensical adventures.

Children who love Dr. Seuss seem to like things that way. And that's just fine, because while they're having fun, laughing at the animals' antics and the people's pranks, they are also learning early language and literacy skills – without even realising it!

So sit with your child and talk and laugh together about what you see. Help your child to match the headwords to the pictures, then find the headwords and other related words in the sentences – they're highlighted in blue to make it easier. Discuss what's going on in the pictures and ask the questions; you can even make up questions of your own. Teach your child the names of the letters and their sounds, and read the alphabet together until your child begins to absorb its rhythm.

At first, you'll find that *you* need to read this dictionary to your child, but after a while it will be *your child* reading it to you!

Aaron

Aa

Aaron is an alligator.

above

Aaron flies above the clouds.

about

Aaron is about to go up.

accident

He's had an accident.
Poor Aaron!

4

across

Abigail goes across.

afraid

Abigail is afraid.

add

Abigail adds up.

again

Aaron is up again.

aeroplane

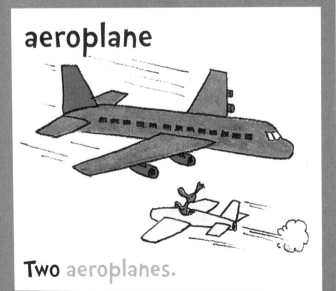

Two aeroplanes.

alone

All alone!

alphabet

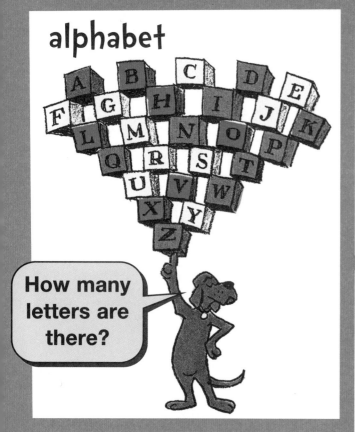

How many letters are there?

another

Another **angry animal.**

answer

Answer **it!** Answer **it!**

always

Aaron is always having accidents!

apple

Arms full of apples.

angry

An angry animal.

arrow

aunt

Abigail's Aunt Ada.

ask

Abigail asks for an apple.

automobile

Aunt Ada's automobile.

asleep

Aaron
is asleep.

Aaron
is awake.

away

Away goes Aunt Ada.

axe

7

baby

B b

Good baby.

back

A baby on a lion's back.

bad

Bad baby.

bake

A baker bakes bread.

ball

Let's play ball.

balloon

Baby likes balloons.

banana

Baby likes bananas.

band

The band plays on.

barber

Aaron goes to the barber.

bath

Time for a bath.

behind

A bear behind a tree.

bear

bell
Ringing bells.

bed

A bear in bed in his bedroom.

beside

A bear beside a tree.

bee

Bees after a bear.

between

A bear between two trees.

bicycle

Aunt Ada's bicycle.

block

What do you build with blocks?

bird

blow

The wind blows.

birthday

A bird's birthday cake.

black

A blackbird at a blackboard.

blue

11

bones

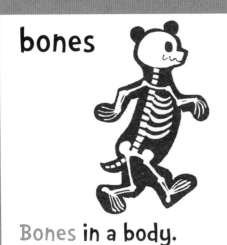

Bones in a body.

book

A book about birds.

bottle

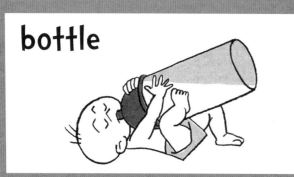

box

Bananas in a box.

breakfast

Breakfast in bed.

brick

Aaron carries bricks.

bridge

Baby in a boat
under a bridge.

bright

A bright light.

brush

Bear brushes his hair.

bucket

How many buckets am I carrying?

build

Builders build a building.

bus

Catch the bus to school.

button

Big blue buttons.

13

C c

cactus

A cowboy caught on a cactus.

call

HERE, CAMEL, CAMEL, CAMEL.

Aunt Ada calls her camel.

cage

A lion in a cage.

camera

CLICK

candle

Carry the candle.

catch

Catch the ball.

cap

We all have caps.

chair

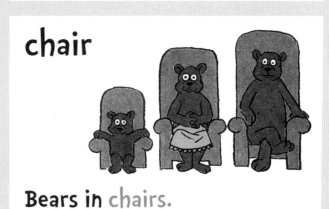

Bears in chairs.

car

car   cart

chase

Aunt Ada chases a fly.

castle

cheese

I love cheese.

15

chicken

A chicken with her chicks.

child

one child   three children

chimney

Santa Claus
goes down the chimney.

chin

Christmas

Merry Christmas!

circle

All in a circle.

clean

Keeping the streets clean.

climb

Climbers climb **the mountain.**

clown

A circus clown.

clock

alarm clock   **cuckoo** clock

coat

Abigail in Aunt Ada's coat.

clothes

Clothes **dry on a** clothesline.

cold

Aaron is cold.

colours

What is your favourite colour?

cook

A cook cooks a cookie.

comb

corn

corn on the cob   popcorn

corner

A mouse in a corner.

come

"Come along!"   He came.

count

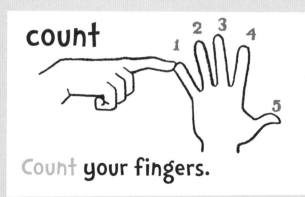

Count your fingers.

18

cow

bull

cow

calf

cry

Baby likes to cry.

crayon

Baby likes crayons.

cup

A cup and saucer.

crow

crown

The king wears a crown.

cut

Aaron cuts the paper.

Dd

dad

Dad is dancing with Aaron.

deep

Deep down.

dark

It's dark at night.

It's light in the day.

dentist

Aaron goes to the dentist.

dive

Aunt Ada dives in.

dinner

Bear cooks dinner.

dinosaur

do

The "do" words

did
does
doesn't
doing
don't
done

dishes

He washes dirty dishes.

doctor

A dog doctor.

dog

WOOF!
WOOF!

The dog barks.

down

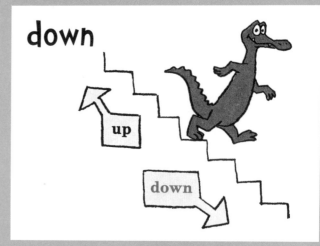

up

down

doll

How much do I cost?

£5

dozen

A dozen doughnuts.

door

"Close that door!"

draw

Baby draws a duck.

dream

Abigail dreams about dresses.

dot

Lots of dots.

drink

A deer drinks water.

dry

She dries her hair.

drip

The drops drip.

dump

Dumping rubbish at the dump.

drum

dust

A cloud of dust.

ear

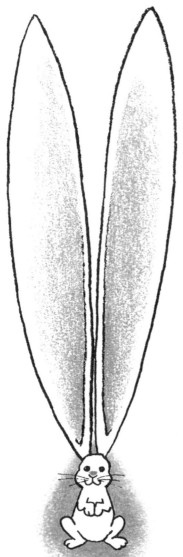

Big ears.

eat

I eat eight eggs.

early

An early bird
catches the worm.

elephant

24

empty

An empty bed.

end

The back end of an elephant.

entrance

every

The "every" words

everyone

everybody

everything

everywhere

exercise

Aunt Ada exercises.

eye

eyebrow

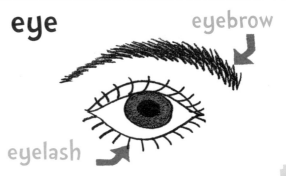

eyelash

fairy

fall

The fairy falls on her face.

family

A large family.

fan

An electric fan.

far

The star is far away.

26

farm

A farmer farming on his farm.

father

That is my father.

fast

fast   faster   fastest

feather

Fine feathers.

How many feathers do I have?

fat

fat bear   thin bear

feed

Feed spinach to the baby.

feet

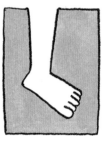

one foot   two feet

fence

Feet on a fence.

few

a few fish

lots of fish

fight

fill

Fill it full.

find

Aaron finds a penny.

fingers

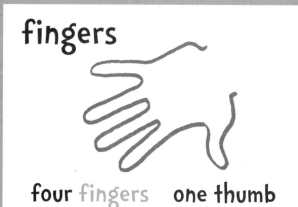

four fingers   one thumb

fire

Firemen **on a** fire **engine.**

fix

"Can you fix **it, Daddy?"**

flag

Flags **on a boat.**

firefly

first

first   second   third

float

Father floats **in the water.**

floor

ceiling

floor

follow

Follow **the leader.**

flower

A big flower.

food

What do you like to eat?

fly

Aaron flies **again.**

fork

knife   fork

found

He found a fox in the forest.

freeze

IT'S FREEZING IN HERE

Deep freeze.

fox

Four foxes.

friend

The frogs are best friends.

free

frown

Gg

game

A game of cards.

giant

Yikes! That giant is tall.

garden

A hippo in the garden.

gift

A gift for the queen.

giraffe

goodbye

goose

one goose   two geese

glasses

Do you wear glasses?

grass

Goats eat grass.

good

good dog   bad dog

grasshoppers

Grasshoppers hopping.

33

grey

Paint the wall grey.

grow

See how tall my flowers grow.

groceries

guess

"Guess who?"

ground

He lives under the ground.

gun

He fires his popgun.

hair

hand

Shaking hands.

ham

A ham sandwich.

hammer

Hammer the
nails in with a hammer.

happy

"Happy birthday to us!"

hat

his hat   her hat

heavy

How much do you weigh?

head

Aunt Ada on her head.

hello

HELLO! WHO'S THERE?

hear

He hears with his ears.

hide

Aaron hides in the barrel.

hit

He hits hard.

hold

Aaron holds the baby.

horse

house

A horse in a house.

hungry

They are hungry.

hurry

"Don't hurry so."

hurt

Now he's hurt himself.

ice cream

Ii

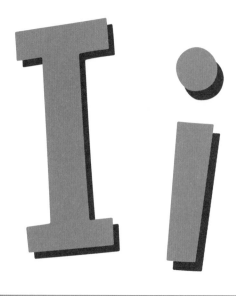

igloo

My igloo is made of snow.

imagine

Imagine what's for lunch.

ice skates

ink

Ink everywhere!

into

Put the
money into the piggy bank.

insect

What kind of
insects are
these?

iron

He irons on an island.

inside

I live inside
a tree.

itch

I itch.

jacket

Jack wears a jacket.

jack-o-lantern

Jack's jack-o-lantern.

jar

James falls in the jam jar.

jam

James likes jam.

jet

Jerry in his jet.

joke

Joe plays a joke on Jack.

jungle

Jerry in the jungle.

juice

Jack likes juice.

junk

jump

James jumps over
Jack and Joe.

Jack, James, Jerry
and Joe in a junk yard.

kangaroo

kick

Aunt Ada kicks the ball.

kettle

The kettle boils.

key

key   keyhole

king

kiss

The king kisses Abigail.

knees

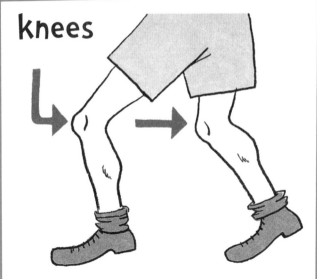

Two knobbly knees.

kite

"Don't fly your kite in here."

knife

"Don't eat with your knife."

kitten

mother cat   kitten

knock

KNOCK KNOCK

Who's that knocking
at my door?

ladder

Aunt Ada up a ladder.

Ll

lamb

My child is a lamb.

lake

Sailing on Lake Minnihaweetonka.

lap

Bears on laps.

lasso

Catch the cow with a lasso.

lazy

We all feel lazy.

late

Late for school again.

learn

Baby bird learns to fly.

laugh

I laugh when I'm happy and cry when I'm sad.

let

"Let me out of here."

letter

Aaron posts a letter.

lick

lie

" Lie down."

He lay down.

lift

Aaron lifts a lot of lemons.

lion

Aunt Ada likes lions.

lip

Hot lips!

listen

Listen to the bird sing.

46

little

little bird   big bird

look

He looks **for his lost sock.**

lollipop

Baby likes lollipops.

love

Who do you love?

She loves **her baby.**

long

long

longer

longest

lunch

Time for lunch.

Mm

machine

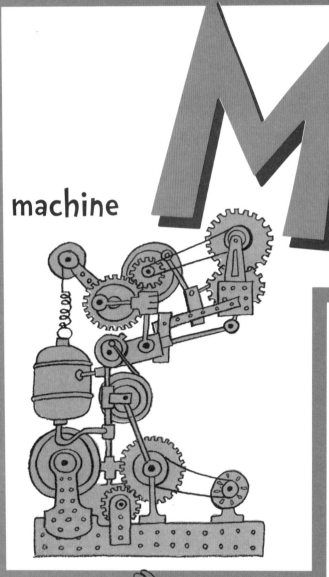

make

Aaron makes another machine.

made

I made it all by myself.

man

four men

one man

mask

A moose mask.

mess

What an awful mess.

mat

A door mat.

midnight

Midnight is the middle of the night.

meat
meet

They meet at the meat counter.

minute

It's five minutes to five.

miss

He's missed the bus.

monkey

A monkey
with a monkey wrench.

mix

Mix the eggs into the flour.

moon

Aaron is going to the moon.

money

Jack has lots more
money than Joe.

morning

What a beautiful morning!

move

They move to another house.

mother

She is my mother.

mud

Aunt Ada is stuck in the mud.

mountain

mountain   hill

music

What instrument do you play?

Making music.

nail

Nn

hear

name

"What's your name?"

I live near Kugluktuk.

neck

Aaron wears
a bow tie round his neck.

never

He will never get me!

need

We need a bath.

new

new shoe   old shoe

nest

At rest in my nest.

newspaper

THE
DAILY NEWS

net

next

"I am next."

night

noodle

Eating noodle soup.

noon

Noon is the middle of the day.

noise

"Stop that noise!"

north

The bird flies north.

none

There is none left.
No. Not a drop.

nose

little nose   big nose

nothing

Nothing **at all.**

now

Can you tell the time?

It is now **four-thirty.**

numbers

hurse

Aaron's hurse.

nut

A coconut. **Ouch!**

oar

ocean

O o

off

Aagh! I fell off.

oil

I oil my bike.

old

An old, old mouse.

ouch

out

I run out of the house and play outside.

open

mouth open   mouth shut

ostrich

Our own ostrich.

over

Jumping over a clover.

other

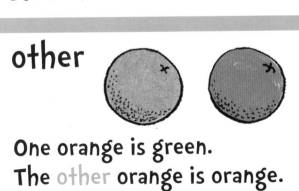

One orange is green.
The other orange is orange.

overalls

Aaron's overalls.

Pp

pack

Aaron packs his suitcase.

page

He turns
the page of his book.

package

Carrying lots of packages.

paint

The dog paints a picture.

pair

What a pretty pair of pyjamas.

parachute

palace

This is my palace.

party

A birthday party.

paper

Here comes the paper boy.

pay

They pay for their tickets.

peanuts

Aaron eats peanuts.

pepper

pepper   salt

pen

pencil   pen

pet

Cats and dogs are good pets.

people

How many people live in your house?

people   animals

phone

They phone from a phone box.

piano

pinch

He's pinching me.

pie

A piece of pie.

pirate

pig

A pink pig on a pillow.

plant

Plant a tree in a pit.

pin

Baby wears a safety pin.

plate

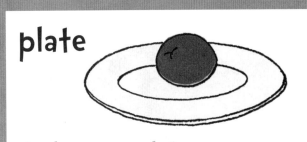

A plum on a plate.

play

They play in the playground.

please

pole

Pole vaulting.

police

I am a police horse.

pony

porpoise

pot

Hot pot.

potato

Hot potato.

prize

puddle

pull

"Pull me out of the puddle."

puppy

Meet my little puppy.

push

Aunt Ada pushes her car.

puzzle

Aaron is puzzled by the puzzle.

quack

QUACK
QUACK
QUACK
QUACK

"Ducks go quack".

quarrel

You must not quarrel!

quarter

The bird eats a quarter of the cake.

queen

Here's the milkman with a bottle of milk for the queen.

quick

"Quick," says the queen.

"Take this milk away quickly."

question

The queen asks a question. "Is this milk fresh?"

"No, queen. It is old milk," answers the milkman.

quiet

The quiet milkman takes the milk away quietly.

rabbit

The rabbits run a race.

rain

The rain rains on the rabbits.

rat

read

ALL ABOUT CHEESE

What do you like to read?

The rat reads a book.

raincoat

The rabbits race in raincoats.

red

Paint it red.

ribbon

Hair ribbons.

refrigerator

Called a fridge **for short.**

rich

The king is rich.

reindeer

There's a reindeer
in our refrigerator.

ride

We ride **on a rhinoceros.**

right

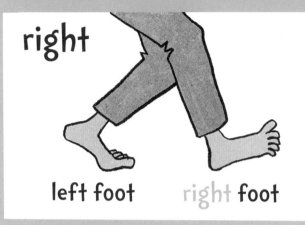

left foot   right foot

rocket

A rocket over rocky mountains.

ring

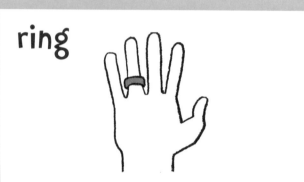

river

Ducks on a river.

roll

Aunt Ada rolls along on roller skates.

road

Ducks on a road.

roof

Now she's roller-skating on the roof.

room

My room is a mess.

row

He rows in a rowing boat.

rope

"Pull. Pull on the rope!"

round

Hoops are round.

run

The running rhinoceros runs to Rochester.

sad

A sad, sad dog.

same

We look alike.
We are the same.

sail

A sailor sails his sailing boat.

sand

Baby plays in the sand.

sandwich

A big sandwich.

saw

I saw **a seesaw.**

sank

His sailing boat sank.

scissors

SNIP

scooter

Aaron rides his scooter.

saw

I see a saw.

scratch

Having a good scratch.

sell

He sells hot dogs.

shake

They shake paws.

send

Mother sends us to bed.

sharp

Needles are sharp.

shadow

Aunt Ada's shadow.

sheep

The sheep bleats.

shell

My house is a shell.

short

This shirt is too short.

shine

My shoes shine.

shout

ship

A ship is a big boat.

sick

Poor Aaron. He feels sick.

73

sign

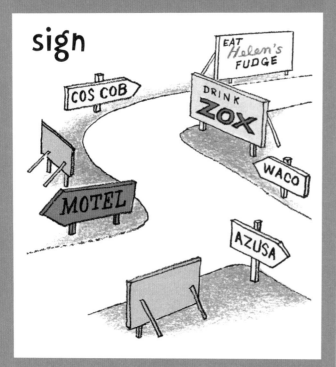

sit

The seven sisters sit down.
They are sitting on a seat.

silly

Pulling a silly face.

skate

A skunk on skates.

sledge

sing

The seven sisters
sing songs.

sleep

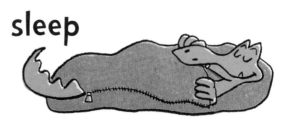

Aaron sleeps soundly
in his sleeping bag.

slide

We slide down the slide.

slow

slow   fast

smell

Skunks smell pongy.

snack

Aaron eats a snack in a shack.

sneeze

The snake sneezes.

snow

snowman

snowball

showshoes

soap

Frothy soapsuds.

sock

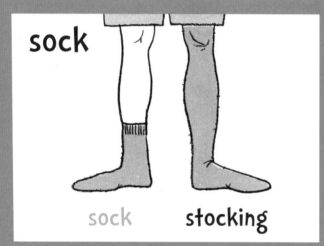

sock   stocking

some

The "some" words.

spell

How do you spell Llewellyn?

spider

A spider's web.

spill

Baby spills the milk.

76

splash

The elephant makes a big splash.

stamp

Lick the stamp to stick it.

spot

They call me spot.

start

Aunt Ada can't start her car.

stairs

Aaron comes down the stairs.

steps

The steps are very steep.

stick

Smart dogs fetch sticks.

sting

Mosquitoes sting.

stone

Rolling stones.

stop

story

Jack reads them a bedtime story.

straight

What's your hair like?

straight hair   curly hair

street

OAK STREET

PINE STREET

string

A long string.

sweater

swim

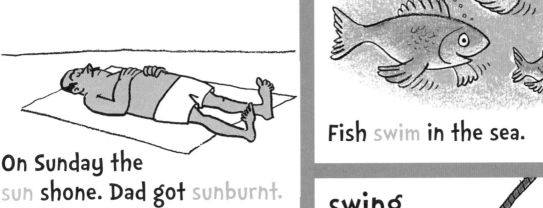

Fish swim in the sea.

sun

On Sunday the sun shone. Dad got sunburnt.

swallow

The ostrich has swallowed four oranges.

swing

We swing on the swing.

Tt

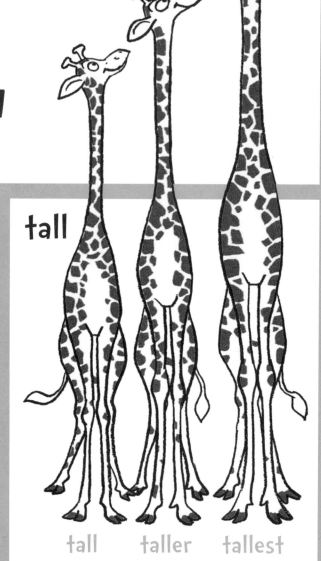

tall

tall   taller   tallest

table

"Take your feet off the table."

tail

A very long tail.

tame

A tame lion with a lion tamer.

taste

This lemon tastes sour.

teach

Their teacher teaches them to sing.

telephone

Talking on the telephone.

television

They like watching television.

tell

"I told you before. I will tell you again. Turn it down!"

tent

Ten boys in a tent.

thank

"Thank you for the tomatoes."

thermometer

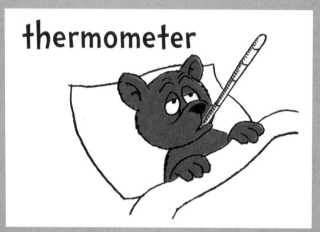

thing

think

A blue thing thinks about a red thing.

threw

He threw it through the window.

throw

"Did you throw this?"

tie

He ties the tiger to a tree.

82

time

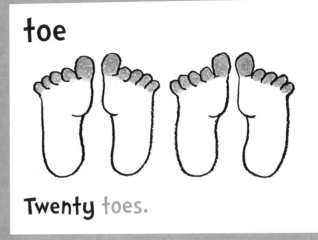

The time is now
twelve minutes to twelve.

toe

Twenty toes.

tired

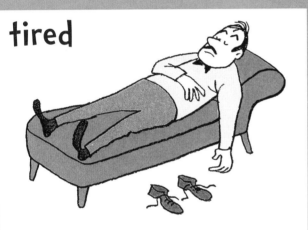

All tired out!

tongue

today

Today is the twelfth.
Tomorrow is the thirteenth.

too

too fat   too thin

tooth

one tooth

lots of teeth

toothbrush

tree

A red thing in a tree.

toy

What are your favourite toys?

Playing with his toys.

trick

My dog does tricks.

train

Trains run on tracks.

trousers

A pair of blue trousers.

truck

A truck full of rabbits.

true

Don't believe him. It's not true.

trunk

An elephant's trunk.

try

I will try to fly.

I shouldn't have tried it.

twins

U u

umbrella

Uncle Uriah is under his umbrella.

underwear

Uncle Uriah is in his underwear.

up

Now he is up a pole.
He is upside down.

us

He makes us laugh.

use

We use him as a horse.

86

valentine

A Valentine card for Aunt Ada.

violin

The dog plays the violin.

vanilla

vanilla   strawberry

volcano

The volcano erupts.

very

A very, very, very small dog.

wag

walrus

A walrus on a wall.

wake

WAKE UP

walk

Two cats walk on a wall.

wash

Aaron washes the baby.

water

Aunt Ada surfs on the water.

whale

A whopping great whale.

wear

The seven sisters wear green hats.

wheel

front wheel   back wheel

weigh

How much do we weigh?

white

white   black

why

He wants to know why.

wing

win

Who will win the race?

wink

Now you try it!

wind

The wind blows through the window.

woman

one woman   three women

won't

"I won't eat it."

world

Aaron flies round the world.

wood

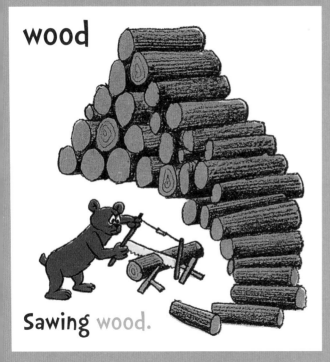

Sawing wood.

write

wrong

His spelling is wrong.

work

It's hard work.

xiphosuran

xylophagous

X x

OH! X WORDS ARE HARD.

xanthophyll

xerophthalmia

DON'T WORRY. HERE ARE SOME EASY ONES.

x-ray

X-rays look inside you.

Xmas

Dancing round the Xmas tree.

xylophone

The dog plays the xylophone.

Yy

yawn

That's a wide yawn.

yellow

Paint it yellow.

yell

I yell. My dog yelps.

yoyo

Aaron plays with his yoyo.

93

zebras

Z z

zip

The zip is stuck.
I can't get out.

zero

Zero is too cold for zebras.

zoo

zyxuzpf

A nest full of zyxuzpf birds. Do you have any in your garden?

The end.